Contents

Acknowledgements

The publisher's thanks are due to the following for permission to use copyright material:

Faber and Faber for W. H. Auden's 'The Sabbath' from *Homage to Clio*, Paul Muldoon's 'Hedgehog' from *New Weather*, Louis MacNeice's 'Jigsaw II' from *Collected Poems* and George Barker's 'On a Friend's Escape from Drowning off the Norfolk Coast' from *Collected Poems*; David Higham Associates for Edwin Brock's 'Five Ways to Kill a Man' from *With Love from Judas*; Angus and Robertson (UK) Ltd for Judith Wright's 'Woman to Child' from *Woman to Man* and Rosemary Dobson's 'Child of our Time' from *Crockcrow*; Zulfikar Ghose for 'The Crows' from *The Loss of India*; the New York Times Company for Zulfikar Ghose's 'Egypt' (© 1965 by the New York Times Company. Reprinted by permission); David Harsent for his poems 'Heart' and 'The Woman and the Cat'; Louis Johnson for his poem 'Bread and a Pension'; Philip Johnstone for his poem 'High Wood'; Evan Jones for his poem 'The Lament of the Banana Man'; Charles Scribner's Sons for 'The Crabs' (copyright © 1962 Richmond Lattimore) reprinted by permission of Charles Scribner's Sons from *Poems of Three Decades* by Richmond Lattimore; George Macbeth for his poem 'Buying a Heart'; The Hogarth Press for Norman MacCaig's 'Solitary Crow' from *Rings on a Tree*; Basil McFarlane for his poem 'I am Jamaica'; Victor Gollancz for Alasdair Maclean's 'Crow' from *From the Wilderness*; Hope Leresche and Steele for Roger McGough's 'Why Patriots Are a Bit Nuts in the Head' from *Penguin Modern Poets*, 10; Michael Joseph for Spike Milligan's 'Unto Us . . .' from *Small Dreams of a Scorpion*; J. M. Dent for Robert Morgan's '4C Boy', 'Listen' and for Herbert Williams' 'Jones the Grocer' from *Welsh Voices*, ed. Bryn Griffiths; Ted Hughes for Sylvia Plath's 'Mirror' from *Crossing the Water* (copyright Ted Hughes 1971, Faber); Routledge and Kegan Paul for Peter Redgrove's 'Early Morning Feed' from *The Collector and Other Poems*; Angus and Robertson for Elizabeth Riddell's 'Life-Saver' from *Forbearers*; Richard Ryan for his poem 'The Thrush's Nest'; Vernon Scannell for his poem 'Incendiary'; Jon Silkin and Chatto and Windus for 'Caring for Animals'; Barbara Noel Scott for her poem 'Stillbirth'; Oxford University Press for Anthony Thwaite's 'Hedgehog' from *The Owl in the Tree*; The Bodley Head for Rex Warner's 'Nile Fishermen' from *Poems* and J. D. Lewis and Sons, Gomer Press, Llandysul Dyfed for Harri Webb's 'Not to be Used for Babies' from *Green Desert*.

To the Teacher

To many people, setting exams on poetry seems like sacrilege. It is as brutal as pulling a butterfly to pieces to see what makes it beautiful. One sympathizes with this view but the fact is that poetry appreciation forms part of the syllabus of many examining boards and that the final exam frequently takes the form of answering questions on an 'unseen' poem.

It is to provide practice in thinking and writing about poetry that this book has been compiled. Discussing a new poem in class can be valuable and stimulating but for many young people there comes a time when they must formulate and write answers to specific questions under exam conditions. Students often find this difficult and it is hoped that the introductory section of this book will prove useful, as well as the list of critical terms to be found at the back. The points made in the introduction are all obvious and ought to be common knowledge but my experience as an examiner has shown that too many candidates lack an adequate critical apparatus and fail to do themselves justice in this part of the exam. Teachers who feel that the advice presented merely reiterates what they have repeated *ad nauseam* have only to tell their classes to skip the next few pages – always a popular instruction.

The poems and questions that form the bulk of the book have, as far as possible, been graded in difficulty and although they are intended mainly for CSE candidates they will provide suitable preliminary practice in a GCE course.

Opportunity has been taken of publication in book form to present the poems in a sequence where individual items complement one another and set up reverberations. Teachers, however, will use the poems in the order and in the way that best suits their own purposes. Some will use them as discussion material rather than for formal exam practice while others will see them primarily as a source of homework assignments.

In whatever way the book is used, I trust that hard-pressed teachers will find that it relieves them, at least in part, from the necessity of devising their own material, a laudable but time-consuming activity.

A.P.

To the Student

Discussing poetry informally in class is one thing: it can be an enjoyable experience to think aloud and grope for the exact words to express our feelings about a particular poem. We can help one another, too, to a fuller realization of what the poet is trying to do. But sooner or later, in these examination-bound days, many of you will be faced with an 'unseen' poem to tackle under exam conditions – a different thing altogether.

You must know what sort of questions to expect and must have at your finger-tips at least some of the technical terms that people use when they are discussing poetry. The informal gropings – 'Well, it's sort of – you know – poetic' – just won't do. A more disciplined approach is needed and this can only come with practice – the sort of practice in reading, thinking and writing that this book aims to provide.

Your teacher, of course, is the best person to guide your appreciation of a poem but in the exam room you are on your own with no one to nudge you along the path to fuller understanding. Think of the questions set on the poems in this book as fulfilling the role formerly played by your teacher. They are meant to draw your attention to important points which can lead you to fuller appreciation. They are not meant merely to provide a framework of comprehension exercises that can be answered more or less mechanically. Their real purpose is to make you think more deeply about the significance of the poem. You then have the problem of communicating your reaction to your reader.

At the back of this book you will find a list of technical terms which will help you in this business of communication. Work through it gradually until you become familiar with the terms listed and then try to apply them when you are answering the questions set. These questions vary in emphasis from poem to poem but there are several basic principles that you can apply when tackling any 'unseen' poem.

First you should read the poem carefully several times. Poetry is often a very rich, compressed kind of writing and if you are to appreciate fully what the poet is getting at, you will have to dig deep. Having taken in what the poem is about, read through the questions that follow so that you have an idea what ground is covered by specific questions. It is important to do this so that you avoid including in an early answer material that would be more relevant in a later one. Make sure, too, that you stick to the numbering of the questions as printed, especially if there are sub-sections such as 1(i) . . . (ii) . . . (iii) or 1 a) . . . b) . . . c). It is very confusing for an examiner trying to mark to a scheme if you use a private one of your own, re-shuffling sub-sections at will.   It is obviously impossible to cover here every question with which you may be faced but most questions fall into five general categories. We will consider these in turn.

First, there are those designed to test whether you have under-stood the poem: questions about meaning nearest in type to the comprehension questions set on prose in language papers. Keep your answers short and to the point and use your own words as far as possible. Incidentally, do have a go at each question, even if you are doubtful about your answer: blank spaces never gain marks.

Second, there are questions which ask you to comment on the poet's choice of words, or which draw your attention to points of poetic technique such as figures of speech. These are devices used by all writers to make their work more vivid and they are a par-ticular feature of poetry. The figures of speech that you will en-counter most frequently are similes and metaphors and you should try to master these as soon as possible. They are ex-plained, along with other important terms, on pages 50–53. There is little merit in merely recognizing a simile or a metaphor: what you must do is to cultivate the ability to comment on their aptness, their effect and the contribution they make to the poem as a whole. Try, too, to develop an 'ear' for poetry, which, ideally, of course, should be heard rather than read. The music of poetry may not come through very clearly in the examination room with the clock on the wall ticking the minutes away, but the more verse you read and the more you analyse particular lines and effects, the easier you will find the whole business of appreciation. Get into the habit of scrutinizing words and phrases and even the different combinations of letters. For ex-ample, what effect is made by the long-drawn-out vowel sounds in words such as *moan, moon* and *mourn*? What impression is created by consonant combinations in such words as *pitter-patter* or *snip-snap*? Begin to value words for their sound as well as for their meaning.

A third type of question may try to test your response to images that the poet has used to set your imagination working. The five senses of sight, hearing, smell, taste and touch are important here. The re-creation of experience and the sharing of private visions are important features of many poems and the wider the range of sense-impressions used, the better chance the poet has of encouraging the response he is looking for. You may be asked for your personal reaction to 'word-pictures' used in the course of a poem and the more experience you gain in this personal sort of writing the better.

A fourth kind of question may ask you to comment on the poem as a whole. You may be asked to discuss the point of view presented or the mood, tone or 'atmosphere' that is built up. One feature which is true of all writing about poetry is particularly relevant here: it is that very often there are no 'right' answers to the questions set. People's reactions to the same poem vary enormously and you are entitled to your own view, provided that it is a reasonable interpretation of the evidence set before you in the poem. You must be prepared to select evidence to support your view and present it as the basis of your answer. This is the purpose behind the injunction which you will find repeated throughout the questions in this book – 'Give your reasons.' Examiners are prepared to consider any viewpoint when it is supported by sound argument firmly based on the text. What they do object to are lazy statements of the 'This poem is a load of rubbish' variety. Such pronouncements say more about the exam candidate than the poem. Even if the poem is hard to understand, you must make the effort and at least attempt to unravel what the poet is trying to put over. You can be assured that no poems presented for detailed criticism in public exams are 'rubbish'. Like the poems in this book, they will have been selected because they have something worthwhile to say to young people today.

A final category of questions widely employed is that involving the comparison of poems or extracts on a similar theme. Here you may be asked to compare and contrast them from various standpoints — language, form, treatment, and so on. You will probably be asked to state which poem you prefer and, once again, your opinion will be respected if the necessary supporting evidence is given.

In conclusion, it cannot be over-emphasized that reading poetry demands more effort than reading prose and that the more you work at a poem, the more you will get out of it. I hope that working through the poems and questions that follow will open your eyes to the surprising power of poetry and perhaps encourage you to go on reading it when you leave school. This would be a much more satisfying result, really, than gaining good marks in your exams, which is no doubt your immediate aim.

1 Unto Us...

Somewhere at sometime
They committed themselves to me
And so, I was!
Small, but I *was*.
5 Tiny in shape
Lusting to live
I hung in my pulsing cave.
Soon they knew of me
My mother – my father.
10 I had no say in my being
I lived on trust
And love.
Tho' I couldn't think
Each part of me was saying
15 A silent 'Wait for me
I will bring you love!'
I was taken
Blind, naked, defenceless
By the hand of one
20 Whose good name
Was graven on a brass plate
in Wimpole Street,
and dropped on the sterile floor
of a foot operated plastic waste bucket.
25 There was no Queen's Counsel
To take my brief.
The cot I might have warmed
Stood in Harrod's shop window.
When my passing was told
30 My father smiled.
No grief filled my empty space.
My death was celebrated
With two tickets to see Danny la Rue
Who was pretending to be a woman
35 Like my mother was.

1 Who is the imaginary narrator of this poem and who are the people referred to as 'they' in line 2?

2 What is the 'cave' mentioned in line 7 and why is it described as 'pulsing'?

3 What is meant by
   'I had no say in my being' (line 10)?

4 Quote the line which marks a sudden change in the tone of the poem.

5 Explain the reference in lines 19–22 to the person with his name on a brass plate.

6 What did this person do?

7 Comment on the reaction of the father and mother (lines 30–31).

8 Explain the significance of the reference to Danny la Rue (lines 32–34).

9 a) What social problem is this poem about?
   b) To judge from the poem, what is the poet's own attitude to this problem?
   c) Explain, with reasons, whether or not you think he has presented his case effectively.

10 a) Mention some arguments that might be advanced on the other side.
   b) Briefly, what are your own views on the subject?

2a Woman to Child

You who were darkness warmed my flesh
where out of darkness rose the seed.
Then all a world I made in me:
all the world you hear and see
hung upon my dreaming blood.

There moved the multitudinous stars,
and coloured birds and fishes moved.
There swam the sliding continents.
All time lay rolled in me, and sense,
and love that knew not its beloved.

O node and focus of the world —
I hold you deep within that well
you shall escape and not escape —
that mirrors still your sleeping shape,
that nurtures still your crescent shell.

I wither and you break from me;
yet though you dance in living light,
I am the earth, I am the root,
I am the stem that fed the fruit,
the link that joins you to the night.

1 Express in your own words what the woman is telling the child in
   the first stanza.
2 What parallel is drawn in the second stanza?
3 Try to explain the apparent contradiction in the third stanza:
                              'that well
       you shall escape and not escape'.
4 Explain the force of the metaphor that is developed in the last
   stanza.

2b   Child of our Time

The world is yours, and you must take
Your making, breathing, shaping way:
That instant when the cord was cut
Ended my brief imperial sway.

Mine only was the being shaped
In darkness and in solitude
Moving upon the tides of dream,
Unknown yet known beatitude.

All that is done. Now every step
You take is further still from me
Along your destined path to death,
Light, darkness or eternity.

Child of an age beyond my dreams,
My comprehension, watch, or care,
Where do you go who may set foot
Upon some distant, radiant star?

All women who since time began
Have trembled for an eager child
Feared dangers fixed and bounded by
The narrow circuit of the world.

I see the wounded moon, I fear
The travelling star, the mushroom cloud,
Beneath the perilous universe
For you, for you, my head is bowed.

5 Who is the narrator of this poem and who is the person
  addressed? How do you know?
6 What stage of human life is described in stanza 3?
7 Explain the references in the last stanza to a) 'the wounded
  moon'; b) 'the travelling star'; c) 'the mushroom cloud'.
8 What new developments might have made the narrator more
  fearful than women of previous ages? Do you think her sense of
  extra fear is justified?
9 What similarities do you detect between 'Woman to Child' and
  'Child of our Time' as regards theme, form, language and
  treatment?
10 In what ways do the points of view expressed in the two poems
   differ?

3 Stillbirth

Labour was normal, a birth, like any other.
But long, for bearing nothing but a stone;
Pushing a stone of pain uphill for hours
Gasping for breath.
5 Hope did not die till later.
I had been heavy, a stagnant pool, no stir
No beat of heart, hands. Then
This cataclysm that seemed to presage life.
But, at the end, no cry.

10 Under the half-death of the chloroform
I heard the nurse laugh, joking with the doctor,
Thinking I could not hear. I knew, then
And a weak rage rose in my throat
That it was mine they looked at and held light.
15 I would have snatched it from them
Carried it in my mouth to my lair
With animal groans, and licked it back to life.

They took it from me, told me, all's for the best
And shut it in a box. What else to do
20 With something, not quite rubbish?
They did it decently,
Washed the cold face with colder drops of pity,
Baptised it for luck,
And put it in the earth where it belonged.

25 I never saw the features I had made,
The hands I had felt groping
For the life I tried to give, and could not.
But still, I sometimes dream I hear it crying
Lost somewhere and unfed,
30 Shut in a cupboard, or lying in the snow,
And I search the night, and call, as though to rescue
Part of myself, from the grave of things undone.

1 a) Explain the significance of the metaphor developed in lines
  2–4. .

  b) How is the idea carried on later in the poem?

2 What other image does the narrator use in the first section to
  describe her physical state? Explain whether or not you find it
  effective.

3 What is meant by 'the half-death of the chloroform' (line 10)?

4 Comment on the attitude of the nurse and the doctor.

5 Explain the meaning of 'not quite rubbish' (line 20).

6 Do you think it was right that the narrator was never shown her
  stillborn child? Give your reasons.

7 What is the narrator's own explanation of her later reaction as
  described in the last five lines of the poem?

8 The situation outlined in 'Stillbirth' is in many ways different
  from that described in the next poem 'Early Morning Feed' and
  yet the two poems have one image in common. Identify this
  image and show that, although the basic idea is the same, each
  poet gives it a different emphasis.

4 Early Morning Feed

The father darts out on the stairs
To listen to that keening
In the upper room, for a change of note
That signifies distress, to scotch disaster,
The kettle humming in the room behind.

He thinks, on tiptoe, ears a-strain,
The cool dawn rising like the moon:
'Must not appear and pick him up;
He mustn't think he has me springing
To his beck and call,'
The kettle rattling behind the kitchen door.

He has him springing
A-quiver on the landing –
For a distress-note, a change of key,
To gallop up the stairs to him
To take him up, light as a violin,
And stroke his back until he smiles.
He sidles in the kitchen
And pours his tea ...

And again stands hearkening
For milk cracking the lungs.
There's a little panting,
A cough: the thumb's in: he'll sleep,
The cup of tea cooling on the kitchen table.

Can he go in now to his chair and think
Of the miracle of breath, pick up a book,
Ready at all times to take it at a run
And intervene between him and disaster,
Sipping his cold tea as the sun comes up?

He returns to bed
And feels like something, with the door ajar,
Crouched in the bracken, alert, with big eyes
For the hunter, death, disaster.

1 Where is the father at the beginning of the poem and where is his son?
2 The father is anxious about his son and yet he does not go to him. Why is this?
3 Which person that one would expect to be involved in the incident described here is not, in fact, mentioned?
4 What associations are created for you by the simile 'To take him up, light as a violin' in the third section?
5 Suggest more precisely what the poet is thinking of in his simile in the final section. Explain whether or not you think the comparison is apt.
6 What process, mentioned several times, serves as a background to the poem? What is the point, do you think, of mentioning it?

7 Can you see any significance in the varying lengths of the sections into which the poem is divided? Give your reasons.
8 Consider the importance of sound effects in this poem.
9 Explain how the poet gives dramatic interest to this simple incident of everyday life.

5 4C Boy

He was passive, one of seven,
With a subnormal gait and a confused
Brain damaged by the evils of home
And the mean cells of heredity.
5 His speech was slow, peculiar,
Asthmatic, his face flushed
With fear imposed by classmates
In quiet corners of playgrounds.
His bitten fingers moved
10 With spastic slowness, his glasses
Pressed against his eyebrows
And his fleshy ears stuck out
Like two discs of pink plasticine.
Words on paper were strange
15 Symbols for his dull eyes
And ripped thoughts. Painting
Was his only source of joy.
When he laboured on rich compositions
His eyes glared over hoghaired
20 Brush and sugar paper.
His work sparkled with colour;
Fantasies from his imagination forced
Black unending lines of tension
Around shimmering abstract shapes.
25 His paintings reminded me of a tropical
Garden full of rainbows and birds
Where the sun shone in lemon yellow
Over a stream flowing with tears of despair.

1 Explain in your own words the reasons given for this boy's backwardness.
2 How did his schoolmates treat him?
3 List the handicaps from which the boy suffered.
4 Comment on the aptness of the simile used to describe the boy's ears (lines 12–13).
5 What can you deduce from the poem about his ability in reading?
6 a) What would you say are the chief characteristics of the boy's painting?
 b) Which individual words convey most vividly the outstanding aspect of his work?
7 What feature of the tropical garden (lines 25–28) best symbolizes the boy's state of mind?
8 What do you think might have been the narrator's relationship with the boy described here? Give your reasons.
9 How would you summarize the narrator's attitude to the boy? (Is he critical? Neutral? Sympathetic? None of these?) Say how you arrived at your conclusion.

6 Incendiary

That one small boy with a face like pallid cheese
And burnt-out little eyes could make a blaze
As brazen, fierce and huge, as red and gold
And zany yellow as the one that spoiled
5 Three thousand guineas worth of property
And crops at Godwin's Farm on Saturday
Is frightening – as fact and metaphor:
An ordinary match intended for
The lighting of a pipe or kitchen fire
10 Misused may set a whole menagerie
Of flame-fanged tigers roaring hungrily.
And frightening, too, that one small boy should set
The sky on fire and choke the stars to heat
Such skinny limbs and such a little heart
15 Which would have been content with one warm kiss
Had there been anyone to offer this.

1 In your own words, write an outline of the incident that has prompted this poem.

2 Comment on the significance of the metaphor in the second line.

3 Which word or phrase used in the description of the blaze seems to you to be particularly vivid? Why is this?

4 What is the point of the image developed in lines 8–11? In what ways is it especially appropriate in this context?

5 a) What does the poet suggest was the reason why the boy started the fire?

  b) In your own words, what does he say would have prevented the blaze?

6 Explain what the poet means when he says that the incident is frightening 'as fact and metaphor' (line 7).

7 Take a close look at 'Incendiary' from the point of view of rhyme, then write a brief comment on this aspect of the poem.

8 Write a paragraph explaining whether or not the poet has aroused your sympathy for this boy.

7 Jones the Grocer

Jones the Grocer, we called him –
A pale man, skilled in servility,
His hands white and soft as the lard he stacked
In small meticulous rows, his head
5 Polished and somehow apologetic, as if
He was crowned forever with dishonour.

I hated him, he was too obsequious by far,
Embellishing transactions with fulsome flattery
Of your habits, your appearance, your miserable opinions.
10 He seemed to exist in a fog
Of self-effacement, through which one caught
The rarest glimpse of a human dignity.

Yet one could suffer the arid washing of his hands
For the joy of that shop, its curiosities,
15 Like the corner where it was always dusk

And equatorial, aromatic with coffee beans,
And calendars derisive of popularity,
And the adverts twenty years out of date.

One could suffer it, and gladly suffer it again
20 To be delivered of this, its successor –
A supermarket, slick and soulless,
Arrogantly accepting the shoppers' homage.

1 What is meant by 'skilled in servility' (line 2)?
2 Comment on the effectiveness of the simile in lines 3 and 4.
3 Explain in your own words why the narrator did not like Jones.
4 What is the poet emphasizing by his reference to 'your miserable opinions' (line 9)?
5 Explain the metaphor that is developed in lines 10–12.
6 What do you think is meant by
   a) 'the arid washing of his hands' (line 13);
   b) 'the corner where it was always dusk
      And equatorial' (lines 15–16)?
7 In what way, according to the poet, does the supermarket differ from Mr Jones's establishment?
8 Quote two examples from the poem of the effective use of alliteration.
9 Write a short paragraph giving your own views on the relative merits and attractions of 'the corner shop' and the self-service supermarket.

8   Not to be Used for Babies

Old Glyn, our milkman, came from down the country
Between Waunarlwydd and Mynydd Bach y Glo,
A neighbour of innumerable uncles and cousins
In an untidy region of marsh and pasture and mines.
5 He spoke Welsh of course, but was frequently too drunk
To talk in any language. His milk, though, was good

And his measure generous, as he splashed it into the jug
From a bright battered can with a big extra splash
For a good boy. The spokes of his light trap
10 And the big brass churn amidships shone in the sun
And his brisk mare Shân was a champion trotter;
And when I took the reins of a Saturday morning
(With Glyn's big paw on them, just in case)
I drove the chariot of the sun, I was Caesar, Ben Hur,
15 I was a big boy, helping the milkman.
My parents said among themselves it was drink,
When Glyn stopped coming. I think it was the bottles
And the new ways, the zombie electric trolley,
The precisely measured pints. Nobody is cheated now,
20 There is nothing extra, splashed out in goodwill
For a good boy. I buy my milk in a tin.
It is a dry powder. They have ground Glyn's bones.

1 What have you learned from the poem about the district where it is set?

2 Using your own words, describe in detail how Old Glyn delivered the milk.

3 Explain the references in line 14 to the chariot of the sun, Caesar and Ben Hur.

4 Why did Glyn stop coming, according to a) the boy and b) the boy's parents?

5 To judge from the poem, what has been gained in a modern milk-round and what has been lost?

6 In your opinion, which particular word from the poem best illustrates the narrator's attitude to modern methods of milk distribution? Why?

7 Comment on the conclusion of the poem from 'I buy my milk in a tin' (line 21). (Is it literally true? What are the narrator's feelings? What does the reference to bones mean?)

8 What has this poem in common with the last one, 'Jones the Grocer'?

9 In what way are the attitudes of the two poets to their subjects different?

9 Listen

Let me tell you this, that down here,
In darkness cracked with light,
We are just as human as you in your
Plush office or wherever you
5 Are with daylight on windows.
We have the same brief heart
With its wrinkle of sin and the same
Mind craving success.
We are not calibans even though
10 We work with brute strength
And crouch in the thin seam
Where water chaps the thigh skin
And the roof strains to close
The gap where we lie.
15 We are charmed by thin mice
Eating crumbs and blind
Flies dancing in the lamps'
Cold light and we are always
Curious of the black, squeezed
20 Roads behind cross-sticks where
Our grandfathers worked as boys.
So if our tongues are blunt and our hands
Screwed by the vice of crude work,
Then remember, these are only grains
25 Hiding the encounter with the soul's landscape.

1 a) Who, do you imagine, is the narrator of this poem?
   b) What gives you that impression?
2 To whom is the poem addressed?
3 Using your own words, explain what qualities the narrator says
   his kind shares with everyone else.
4 Caliban appears in Shakespeare's play *The Tempest*. To judge
   from the reference in line 9, what sort of character do you think
   he is?
5 Explain what is meant by
               'the roof strains to close
      The gap where we lie.' (lines 13–14)

6 Give reasons why a) the mice are described as 'thin' (line 15); b) the flies are said to be 'blind' (line 16); c) the lamplight is described as 'cold' (line 18).

7 What are the

'black, squeezed
Roads behind cross-sticks'

mentioned in lines 19–20 and why are they so described?

8 Try to explain what is meant by the last four lines of the poem.

9 a) What, would you suggest, was the poet's intention in writing this poem?

   b) How successful has he been in achieving it? Give your reasons.

10 a   The Poplar Field

The poplars are fell'd; farewell to the shade
And the whispering sound of the cool colonnade;
The winds play no longer and sing in the leaves,
Nor Ouse on his bosom their image receives.

Twelve years have elapsed since I first took a view
Of my favourite field, and the bank where they grew:
And now in the grass behold they are laid,
And the tree is my seat that once lent me a shade.

The blackbird has fled to another retreat,
Where the hazels afford him a screen from the heat;
And the scene where his melody charm'd me before
Resounds with his sweet-flowing ditty no more.

My fugitive years are all hasting away,
And I must ere long lie as lowly as they,
With a turf on my breast and a stone at my head,
Ere another such grove shall arise in its stead.

'Tis a sight to engage me, if anything can,
To muse on the perishing pleasures of man;
Though his life be a dream, his enjoyments, I see,
Have a being less durable even than he.

1 Say in your own words what the poet tells us in the first stanza that he will miss, now the poplars have been cut down.
2 What can you deduce from the poem about the location of the trees before they were felled?
3 What additional reason has the poet for regretting that the trees are gone?
4 Explain the significance of
   'With a turf on my breast and a stone at my head' (stanza 4).

10 b Binsey Poplars

My aspens dear, whose airy cages quelled,
Quelled or quenched in leaves the leaping sun,
All felled, felled, are all felled;
   Of a fresh and following folded rank
        Not spared, not one
        That dandled a sandalled
      Shadow that swam or sank
On meadow and river and wind-wandering
      weed-winding bank.

O if we but knew what we do
     When we delve or hew –
  Hack and rack the growing green!
     Since country is so tender
  To touch, her being so slender,
  That like this sleek and seeing ball
  But a prick will make no eye at all,
  Where we, even where we mean
     To mend her we end her,
   When we hew or delve:
After-comers cannot guess the beauty been.
   Ten or twelve, only ten or twelve
    Strokes of havoc únselve
     The sweet especial scene,
    Rural scene, a rural scene,
    Sweet especial rural scene.

5 What can we infer about the location of this second group of trees before they were felled?

6 Explain in your own words what the poet thinks about the way we treat nature.

7 a) What parallel does he draw to emphasize the dangers of mistreating 'the growing green'?

  b) Do you find the parallel helpful in understanding the poet's ideas? Give your reasons.

8 Consider the use of rhyme and repetition in this poem and say what they contribute to the overall effect, quoting examples to show what you mean.

9 Although both of these poems spring from similar situations, the writers go on to speculate in different directions. Show how the conclusions reached by each poet show a significant difference.

10 a) Compare and contrast the form, language and mood of the two poems.

  b) Explain with reasons whether you find one poem more effective than the other.

11   The Thrush's Nest

Bramble, like barbed wire,
Stitches the thicket tight, laces
A net of leaves against the
Sun: only the birds can pass.

5 Pinned high where the twigs
Cross, it shapes from a blur;
Still heart of the bush, darkness
Parts slowly to let it through.

Her black pebble-eyes dazed
10 With waiting, the mother snaps
Alive at my presence, grabs
Air, screaming — reveals her shining

Hoard: luminous with heat,
Four freckled ovals of perfect
15 Sky, the skin of one threaded
With cracks – pulsing with life.

1 Why do you think the bramble is compared with barbed wire in line 1?
2 a) Explain the metaphor developed in the first stanza.
  b) Which are the key words used?
3 a) What is described as being
     'Pinned high where the twigs
     Cross' (lines 5–6)?
4 Explain the meaning of a) 'it shapes from a blur' (line 6) and b)
                                 'darkness
     Parts slowly to let it through' (lines 7–8).
5 What is the mother bird waiting for?
6 a) Explain what is meant by
     'Four freckled ovals of perfect
     Sky' (lines 14–15).
  b) Why are they described in these terms?
  c) Why are they 'luminous with heat' (line 13)?
7 Explain in your own words the meaning of the last two lines.
8 a) Of all the metaphors used in this poem, which seems to you the most effective?
  b) What picture does it create in your mind's eye?

12 The Woman and the Cat

Something mnemonic
in the way
it lies:

body slack as rags,
5 a look
of satiety – except

for the crushed
head, the raw
excrescence at

10 the gaping jaw –
rubbery bleb
of its own

congealing guts.
She moves
15 in closer to the kerb-

side, wanting
the sight to print
on her retina:

details, like the way
20 its fur
is slightly ruffled

but still clean,
the outstretched legs,
the tail's shape.

25 She imagines the
small detonations, grind
of bones inside

the splintering
skull, guessing
30 that the eyes went first,

with a soft
crack, like
a trodden grape.

1 'Mnemonic' (line 1) is an unusual word which is pronounced as
though the first letter did not exist – *nemonic*. Its rough meaning

here is 'memorable'. What was there about the incident described in this poem, do you think, which made it stick in the memory?

2 a) Comment on the effectiveness of the simile 'body slack as rags' (line 4).

b) Quote one other simile from the poem and comment on its force and effect.

3 a) What is the dominant impression given by lines 7–13?

b) Explain how the choice of words emphasizes that impression.

4 In your own words, explain why the woman moves in to get a closer look at the cat.

5 Show how sound impressions are used to good effect in lines 25–33.

6 What can you deduce from the poem about how the cat died?

7 Comment on the woman's reaction to the sight of the dead cat.

8 Have you ever had an experience similar to that described here? If so, give brief details and explain what your own reactions were at the time. If not, say what you imagine your reactions would be in similar circumstances.

13   Caring for Animals

I ask sometimes why these small animals
With bitter eyes, why we should care for them.

I question the sky, the serene blue water,
But it cannot say. It gives no answer.

5 And no answer releases in my head
A procession of grey shades patched and whimpering,

Dogs with clipped ears, wheezing cart horses
A fly without shadow and without thought.

Is it with these menaces to our vision
10 With this procession led by a man carrying wood

We must be concerned? The holy land, the rearing
Green island should be kindlier than this.

Yet the animals, our ghosts, need tending to.
Take in the whipped cat and the blinded owl;

15 Take up the man-trapped squirrel upon your shoulder.
Attend to the unnecessary beasts.

From growing mercy and a moderate love
Great love for the human animal occurs.

And your love grows. Your great love grows and grows.

1 What reason can you suggest for the animals' eyes being
described as 'bitter' (line 2)?
2 Why do you think the poet addresses his question about the
animals to 'the sky, the serene blue water' in particular?
3 Explain as fully as you can what the poet means by his reference
to
  'this procession led by a man carrying wood' (line 10).
  (Has it any connection with the procession mentioned in line 6? Is
  the naming of 'The holy land' (line 11) relevant here?)
4 What do you take 'the rearing/Green island' (lines 11–12) to be?
5 Why do you think the animals in lines 14–16 are referred to as
'unnecessary beasts'?
6 What does the poet suggest will be the ultimate effect of caring
for animals?
7 a) For what reason do you think the poet abandons the previous
     pattern of his poem in the last line?
  b) What effect does this last line have?
8 Using as your starting-points this poem and the previous one,
'The Woman and the Cat', write a paragraph explaining your
own attitude to the way we humans, deliberately or accidentally,
treat animals.

14a Hedgehog

The snail moves
Like a hovercraft,
Held up by a rubber
Cushion of itself, sharing its secret

5 With the hedgehog. The hedgehog
Shares its secret with no one.
We say, 'Hedgehog, come out
Of yourself and we will love you.

We mean no harm. We want
10 Only to listen to what
You have to say. We want
Your answers to our questions.'

The hedgehog gives nothing
Away, keeping itself to itself.
15 We wonder what a hedgehog
Has to hide, why it so distrusts.

We forget the God
Under this crown of thorns.
We forget that never again
20 Will a God trust in the world.

1 What is the point of the simile used in the first stanza?
2 What is meant by
'Hedgehog, come out
Of yourself' (lines 7–8)?
3 a) Explain the references to 'God' and 'crown of thorns' in lines
17–18.
b) What connection does the poet imply that they have with a
hedgehog?
4 Why is it suggested that
'never again
Will a God trust in the world' (lines 19–20)?

14b Hedgehog

Twitching the leaves just where the drainpipe clogs
In ivy leaves and mud, a purposeful
Creature at night about its business. Dogs
Fear his stiff seriousness. He chews away

5 At beetles, worms, slugs, frogs. Can kill a hen
With one snap of his jaws, can taunt a snake
To death on muscled spines. Old countrymen
Tell tales of hedgehogs sucking a cow dry.

But this one, cramped by houses, fences, walls,
10 Must have slept here all winter in that heap
Of compost, or have inched by intervals
Through tidy gardens to this ivy bed.

And here, dim-eyed, but ears so sensitive
A voice within the house can make him freeze,
15 He scuffs the edge of danger; yet can live
Happily in our nights and absences.

A country creature, wary, quiet and shrewd,
He takes the milk we give him, when we're gone.
At night, our slamming voices must seem crude
20 To one who sits and waits for silences.

5 What is meant by
'Dogs
Fear his stiff seriousness' (lines 3–4)?
6 In what way is this hedgehog out of his element?
7 Which of the hedgehog's five senses is given prominence in this
poem? Quote one piece of evidence to show how acute it is.
8 a) Select two phrases from the poem which vividly describe
different aspects of the hedgehog and say what pictures they
bring to mind.
b) Which phrase from the last stanza is particularly effective in

conveying the impact which humans must have on a creature like the hedgehog? Why is the phrase so effective?

9 Show how the use of details helps the reader to visualize the setting of this poem.

10 Explain in detail how these two poems about the same subject treat it in very different ways.

11 Which of the two poems do you find the more interesting? Briefly explain why.

15 The Sabbath

Waking on the Seventh Day of Creation
   They cautiously sniffed the air:
The most fastidious nostril among them admitted
   That fellow was no longer there.

5 Herbivore, parasite, predator scouted,
   Migrants flew fast and far—
Not a trace of his presence: holes in the earth,
   Beaches covered with tar,

Ruins and metallic rubbish in plenty
10   Were all that was left of him
Whose birth on the Sixth had made of that day
   An unnecessary interim.

Well, that fellow had never really smelled
   Like a creature that would survive:
15 No grace, address or faculty like those
   Born on the First Five.

Back, then, at last on a natural economy,
   Now his Impudence was gone,
Looking exactly like what it was,
20   The Seventh Day went on,

Beautiful, happy, perfectly pointless ...
   A rifle's ringing crack
Split their Arcadia wide open, cut
   Their Sabbath nonsense short.
25 For whom did they think they had been created?
   That fellow was back,
More bloody-minded than they remembered,
   More god-like than they thought.

1 Why do you think this poem is called 'The Sabbath'?
2 From whose point of view is it written?
3 a) Explain what is meant by 'The most fastidious nostril among them' (line 3).
   b) Which later lines echo this idea?
4 Who is 'that fellow' referred to throughout the poem?
5 Which individual words reflect by their sound the change in mood evident in the last seven lines of the poem? How would you explain the effect they have?
6 What does the poet mean when he describes 'that fellow' as 'bloody-minded' and 'god-like' (lines 27–28)?
7 In your own words, give examples of how this poem jumps about in time.
8 a) What seems to you to be the poet's aim in 'The Sabbath'?
   b) Explain the method he has used to put his ideas across.
   c) Giving your reasons, estimate how successful he has been.

16   The Lament of the Banana Man

Gal, I'm tellin' you, I'm tired fo' true,
Tired of Englan', tired o' you.
But I can't go back to Jamaica now ...

I'm here in Englan', I'm drawin' pay,
5 I go to the underground every day –

Eight hours is all, half-hour fo' lunch,
M' uniform's free, an' m' ticket punch –
Punchin' tickets not hard to do,
When I'm tired o' punchin', I let them through.

10 I get a paid holiday once a year.
Ol' age an' sickness can't touch me here.
I have a room of m'own, an' a iron bed,
Dunlopillo under m'head,
A Morphy-Richards to warm de air,
15 A formica table, an easy chair.
I have summer clothes, an' winter clothes,
An' paper kerchiefs to blow m'nose.

My yoke is easy, my burden is light,
I know a place I can go to any night.
20 Dis place Englan'! I'm not complainin',
If it col', it col', if it rainin', it rainin'.
I don't min' if it's mostly night,
Dere's always inside, or de sodium light.
I don't min' white people starin' at me,
25 Dey don' want me here? Don't is deir country?
You won' catch me bawlin' any homesick tears,
If I don' see Jamaica for a t'ousan' years!

... Gal, I'm tellin' you, I'm tired fo' true,
Tired of Englan', tired o' you,
30 I can't go back to Jamaica now –
But I'd want to die there, anyhow.

1 Who is the narrator of this poem and whom is he addressing?
2 What is his job and what is his attitude to it?
3 Why do you think he says
   'Ol' age an' sickness can't touch me here' (line 11)?
4 What impression is given by the list of possessions in lines 12–17?
5 Summarize in your own words the narrator's attitude to England
   as expressed in lines 20–27.
6 What is his attitude to Jamaica?

7 Write a short paragraph on the narrator's state of mind.

8 a) How has the poet tried to convey through his style of writing that the narrator is a West Indian?

   b) How successful has he been, in your opinion, in creating this character? Give reasons for what you say.

9 Comment on the poet's use of rhyme and repetition and explain whether or not you think they contribute to the effectiveness of the poem.

17   I am Jamaica

I am Jamaica –
And I have seen my
   children grow
Out of their separate
5   truths;
Out of the absolute
   truth of me:
Out of my soil
Into false shadows.
10 And I have wept
So
That the strangers with sunglasses
And red faces
Who survey my passive
15   sorrow
Call me beautiful
And Isle of Springs.
And God!
I have no voice
20 To shout out my
   disgust
When their vile trappings
   brush my skin:
Their filthy coppers
25 Reach my children's
   palms:

These palms: my flesh,
My flesh beloved
But where, oh where
30   my spirit;
Where my self, my fire?
Lost, I wander
     through a sunlit night
Beseeching, beseeching my
35   belly's result
To turn from other Gods
To turn on me
The dawn
Of their regard.

1 Explain in your own words what Jamaica is complaining about in
  the first nine lines.
2 a) Who are the strangers referred to in line 12?
  b) How do you know?
3 Show the connection between the phrases 'I have wept', 'my
  passive sorrow' and 'Isle of Springs' (lines 10–17).
4 a) Put into your own words Jamaica's grounds of complaint
  against the strangers.
  b) Which individual words suggest most vividly the strength of
  Jamaica's feelings about these strangers?
5 a) What is odd about the reference to 'a sunlit night' (line 33)?
  b) Suggest what it might mean.
6 Explain in your own words what Jamaica wants her children to
  do in the last four lines of the poem.
7 Make a list of all the references in the poem which suggest that
  Jamaica is a living being.
8 Do you find that this personification of a country is effective?
  Give your reasons.
9 Give a brief outline of what you imagine would be Jamaica's reaction to the Banana Man of the last poem, who had emigrated to
  England.

18 Jigsaw II

Property! Property! Let us extend
Soul and body without end:
A box to live in, with airs and graces,
A box on wheels that shows its paces,
5 A box that talks or that makes faces,
And curtains and fences as good as the neighbours'
To keep out the neighbours and keep us immured
Enjoying the cold canned fruit of our labours
In a sterilized cell, unshared, insured.

10 Property! Property! When will it end?
When will the Poltergeist ascend
Out of the sewer with chopper and squib
To burn the mink and the baby's bib
And cut the tattling wire to town
15 And smash all the plastics, clowning and clouting,
And stop all the boxes shouting and pouting
And wreck the house from the aerial down
And give these ingrown souls an outing?

1 What are the various boxes referred to in lines 3–5?
2 Which of them are mentioned again later in the poem?
3 What double purpose is served by the curtains and fences?
4 a) Explain what the poet means by 'the cold canned fruit of our labours' (line 8).
   b) Why do you think he chose this particular image?
5 Do you think the poet approves of the destruction caused by the Poltergeist (a mischievous spirit)? Give your reasons.
6 What is 'the tattling wire to town' (line 14)?
7 Explain how rhythm and rhyme play their part in the total effect of this poem.
8 Express in your own words the poet's objections to present-day society as represented in this poem.
9 Explain whether or not you agree with his sentiments.

19 Egypt

Descending towards Cairo, an arid
plain is like a twisted mirror, its haze
the diffused image of the sun. Egypt
is straw to the sun's flame, its monuments
5 are slipping into the floodwaters like beasts
come to drink from the dry interior.

Cranes, absurd as science fiction creatures, stand
where slaves once tore their muscles so that kings
might lie entombed in cool, musk-smelling darkness,
10 mummified, perfect as butterfly specimens:
the more advanced a civilization,
the subtler the refinement of vanity.

The same old Egypt holds its sun-wearied earth
together with transfusions from the Nile,
15 the dammed-up waters a bank of the country's blood.
The concrete lifts its pharaoh head above
the people in Cairo, compelling submission
to the hours of work. The sky is a scrap of iron.

A scholar hurries to a museum,
20 a tourist points his zoom lens at flies
sticking to a cluster of dates in a bazaar.
Second-hand vision records Egypt, myths
endure. The same old Egypt contracts like
a dried fig in the heat of the jet's ascent.

1 What is the situation of the poet at the beginning of this poem?
2 Why do you think the cranes are described as 'absurd' in line 7?
3 What is the poet referring to in lines 8–10?
4 Put into your own words the comment made in lines 11–12.
5 a) Explain the image that the poet uses in lines 13–14.
  b) How is the metaphor carried a stage further in line 15?
6 Comment on the aptness of the expression 'its pharoah head' (line
  16).

7 What do you think the poet means by
   'The sky is a scrap of iron' (line 18)?
8 How is the poem neatly rounded off in the last line?
9 Show in detail how the poet uses similes to enrich the listener's or
   reader's mental picture of Egypt.
10 Outline briefly the impression of Egypt that you have gained
   from this poem.

20   Nile Fishermen

Naked men, fishing in Nile without a licence,
kneedeep in it, pulling gaunt at stretched ropes.
Round the next bend is the police boat and the officials
ready to make an arrest on the yellow sand.

The splendid bodies are stark to the swimming sand
taut to the ruffled water, the flickering palms,
yet swelling and quivering as they tug at the trembling ropes.
Their faces are bent along the arms and still.

Sun is torn in coloured petals on the water,
the water shivering in the heat and the north wind;
and near and far billow out white swollen crescents,
the clipping wings of feluccas, seagull sails.

A plunge in the turbid water, a quick joke stirs
a flashing of teeth, an invocation of God.
Here is food to be fetched and living from labour.
The tight ropes strain and the glittering backs for the haul.

Round the bend comes the police boat. The men scatter.
The officials blow their whistles on the golden sand.
They overtake and arrest strong bodies of men
who follow with sullen faces, and leave their nets behind.

1 What impression do you gain from the poem of the fishermen themselves?
2 Describe in detail the method of fishing used by the men.
3 Identify two metaphors from the third stanza and comment on their effectiveness.
4 Show how the poet makes effective use of a) colour and b) alliteration.
5 How is a sense of tension built up in this poem?
6 Describe in your own words the setting of the poem.
7 Giving your reasons, explain whether you feel any sympathy for the fishermen after reading the poem.
8 Explain in detail which you find more interesting – the wide-ranging bird's eye view of Egypt seen in the previous poem, 'Egypt', or the more restricted water-level viewpoint of 'Nile Fishermen'.

21 Buying a Heart

I consider: that, if she were to
take it out of the deep-freeze less than
bone-hard, frozen muscle, it would prick

my conscience, bleed through newsprint, and be
5 a burden; but that, as things are, though
it ran the blood of an ox for two

years, and weighs nearly half of what will
eat it, now that it is no longer
a pump, and chills my fist, I have to

10 accept the disquieting thought of
inevitable change, whether I
like it or not; and that, even if

my own slow heart, which is a pretty
doubtful affair, were to beat faster
15 in frightened sympathy, there is just

nothing this one could do about it
at all, since it is now entirely
dead. It has a new destiny, which

is to grow wet in the sun, stay cold
20 in another refrigerator
and satisfy one cat for one week.

1 a) Who is the 'she' referred to in line 1?
  b) What exactly is 'it', mentioned in line 2?
  c) What is the connection between them?
2 Explain what the poet means by
                      'it would prick
    my conscience, bleed through newsprint, and be
    a burden' (lines 3–5).
3 Why do you think the poet finds disquieting the 'thought of inevitable change' (lines 10–11)?
4 For what reason might the poet's own heart
                      'beat faster
    in frightened sympathy' (lines 14–15)?
5 Explain in your own words what is the 'new destiny' referred to
  in line 18.
6 What was your reaction to the last line of the poem when you
  first heard or read it? Quote something the poet said earlier
  which foreshadowed this ending.
7 Write a short paragraph commenting on the structure and style
  of 'Buying a Heart'. Do you think it is a poem at all, or is it prose
  which is set out to look like a poem?
8 Giving evidence from the text, explain whether you think the
  writer is here describing an unimportant domestic incident or
  whether he sees the heart as a symbol of something more
  profound.

22 Heart

Nights I've listened to
your soft

throb, red plexus,
the occasional

5 mild clonic quirk
or missed

beat. How your job
must bore

you: the tedious
10 business of pumping.

I dream drub
of hooves, explosions, sough of wing-beats, floods,

flickers of crimson
light, and wake

15 with your
howl clogging

my ears.
Hatred or fear

or lust – it is
20 the same to you.

Each day your anxious rhythm preoccupies me more;
old scars

I had forgotten
start to itch.

25 Trite emblem;
    stupid machine;

    tumid fruit; you
    plod on.

1 In the first seven lines what does the narrator say he has
sometimes done at night?
2 What effect do his dreams have on his heart?
3 Show what is meant by the statement
    'Hatred or fear
    or lust – it is
    the same to you' (lines 18–20).
4 Explain the significance of the expressions 'trite emblem' and
'stupid machine' (lines 25—26).
5 The poet seems to delight in employing unusual words. Select
three that are unfamiliar to you and speculate on their meaning.
6 Write a few lines on the poet's use of sound effects in this poem.
(Pay particular attention to his use of consonants.)
7 Comment on the form of this poem. Do you think it is
appropriate to the subject? (Consider especially the length of
line.)
8 In what ways is this poem similar to the preceding one, 'Buying a
Heart'? In what ways is it different?

23 The Crabs

There was a bucket full of them. They spilled,
crawled, climbed, clawed: slowly tossed
and fell: precision made: cold iodine colour of their own
world of sand and occasional brown weed, round stone
5 chilled clean in the chopping waters of their coast.
One fell out. The marine thing on the grass
tried to trundle off, barbarian and immaculate and to be
killed
With his kin. We lit water: dumped the living mass
10 in: contemplated tomatoes and corn: and with the good
cheer of civilized man,
cigarettes, that is, and cold beer, and chatter,
waited out and lived down the ten-foot-away clatter
of crabs as they died for us inside their boiling can.

1 What is the situation at the beginning of this poem?
2 Comment on the poet's choice of words in
            'They spilled,
    crawled, climbed, clawed: slowly tossed
    and fell' (lines 1–3).
3 Say in your own words what impression is created, in lines 3–5, of the world the crabs normally inhabit.
4 Which two expressions emphasize that the crabs are out of their element on land?
5 What is the effect of printing 'killed' on its own (line 8)?
6 What would you say is the narrator's attitude to the boiling of the crabs? Quote and comment on the expression which seems to you to indicate best what his real feelings are.
7 Give two examples from the poem of the writer's ability to pack a lot of meaning into a few words.
8 Write a paragraph commenting in detail on the form and language of 'The Crabs'. (Is it as casual as it looks? Is any use made of rhyme? Does the poet employ figures of speech?)

24 a Crow

Crow, crow, crow. Was here on the first day.
Flew around, waiting for the crust to cool.
Did not evolve. Started off this way.

Gets fatter as the world gets leaner.
5 Eats carrion, adders, frogs, what have you.
A sort of airborne vacuum-cleaner.

Knocks limpets off rocks. Cracks
lobster claws. Bill is the hardest substance known.
You could use a dead crow for a pickaxe.

10 Played truant when they gave out pity.
Takes the eyes from a sheep in labour.
Sober-suited. Would do well in the City.

Roars with laughter at a snare. Knows a trick
worth two of that. Won't come near an armed man.
15 Can tell a shotgun from a walking-stick.

Our parish records list one ancient kill,
staked down at a crossroads late at night.
A neighbour keeps a feather as an heirloom still.

1 What is the effect of the repetition in the first line?
2 In your own words, summarize the crow's feeding habits.
3 a) What is meant by 'sober-suited' (line 12)?
   b) Why do you think the poet says that the crow would do well in
     the City?
4 In your opinion, what is the significance or implication of the
  final stanza?
5 What impression of the crow have you gained from this poem?
6 a) What is the poet's own attitude to the crow, do you think?
   b) How does the style in which the poem is written help to con-
     vey his attitude? Use quotations to show what you mean.

24 b Solitary Crow

Why solitary crow? He in his feathers
Is a whole world of crow — of a dry-stick nest,
Of windy distances where to be crow is best,
Of tough-guy clowning and of black things done
To a sprawled lamb whose blood beads in the sun.

Sardonic anarchist. Where he goes he carries,
Since there's no centre, what a centre is,
And that is crow, the ragged self that's his.
Smudged on a cloud, he jeers at the world then halts
To jeer at himself and turns two somersaults.

He ambles through the air, flops down and seesaws
On a blunt fencepost, hiccups and says Caw.
The sun glints greasy on his working craw
And adds a silver spot to that round eye
Whose black light bends and cocks the world awry.

7 Which characteristic of a crow is given particular emphasis in
   this second poem?
8 Select two descriptive details which seem to you to be particularly
   vivid and describe the pictures they create in your mind's eye.
9 In what ways does 'Solitary Crow' reinforce what the first poem
   had to say?
10 Which of these two poems do you find more effective? Give your
   reasons and quote as necessary.

24c The Crows

Crows will stick their beaks into anything.
Ugliness protects them: children don't care
to pet them, and when they descend on trees,
eagles discreetly go somewhere quieter.

They will sit on balconies and appear
to comment on passing traffic. Their black
cloak never conceals the dagger of speech,
their communal weapon. They talk, talk, talk.

I've heard them break the silence of night
with sudden loud cawing as if provoked
into dispute by a falling star,
and then flying skywards as though to look

up some evidence, keen as scientists;
yet really, when you see their missions
come mostly to nothing, they appear more
like intensely dedicated politicians.

11 In what ways does this third poem confirm what was said about crows in the first two?

12 How is its point of view different? (Does the title provide a clue? What about the setting? Is the poet saying something about people as well as birds?)

25 Mirror

I am silver and exact. I have no preconceptions.
Whatever I see I swallow immediately
Just as it is, unmisted by love or dislike.
I am not cruel, only truthful —
5 The eye of a little god, four-cornered.
Most of the time I meditate on the opposite wall.
It is pink, with speckles. I have looked at it so long
I think it is a part of my heart. But it flickers.
Faces and darkness separate us over and over.

10 Now I am a lake. A woman bends over me,
Searching my reaches for what she really is.
Then she turns to those liars, the candles or the moon.
I see her back, and reflect it faithfully.
She rewards me with tears and an agitation of hands.
15 I am important to her. She comes and goes.
Each morning it is her face that replaces the darkness.
In me she has drowned a young girl, and in me an old
   woman
Rises toward her day after day, like a terrible fish.

1 Explain what is meant by
   'I have no preconceptions' (line 1).
2 Why is the word 'unmisted' (line 3) particularly apt in this
   context?
3 What is the idea behind the metaphor in line 5?
4 Explain in your own words why the wall is said to flicker (line 8).
5 What can you deduce from the first section about the shape and
   location of the mirror?
6 Show how the new metaphor in line 10 is sustained throughout
   the second section.
7 What reason can you suggest for the candles and the moon being
   called liars in line 12?
8 What exactly is meant by
   'In me she has drowned a young girl' (line 17)?

9 Comment on the force of the finale simile in line 19.

10 Write a short paragraph outlining your reaction to this poem. In particular, explain whether you find effective the way in which an inanimate object is brought to life and given the power to communicate.

26 Life-Saver

He was brought up out of the sea,
His tall body dead.
He was carried shoulder high
Between the sun and the sky.
5 The sun and the water trembled down
From his fingers and from the brown
Valley between his shoulders; and the spray
Fell before him as he passed on his way.

His eyes were dead, and his lips
10 Closed on death, and his feet
Chained with death, and his hands
Cold with death. He is one now with ships
And the bones of pirate bands
Steeped in salt and knavery.
15 One with fish and weed and pearl
And the long lonely beat
Of the waves that curl
On shell and rock and sand
Of a deep drowned land.

20 He was carried shoulder high
Up the alleys of the sun;
And the heat
Washed him over from his head to his feet,
But you cannot give the body back breath
25 With a flagon full of sun.
He is drowned, the tall one.
Thin brother Death
Has him by the throat
On the sand, in the sun.

1 What is ironical about the title of this poem?
2 Describe in your own words what is happening to the life-saver in the first section.
3 What is the effect of the repetition in lines 9–12?
4 What is meant by the reference to the life-saver's being 'one now' with all the things mentioned in lines 13–19?
5 Consider the effect of the rhythm in lines 15–19. What impression do you think the poet is trying to build in the reader's or listener's mind?
6 a) What unusual association of words is found in lines 22–3?
   b) How is the idea carried a stage further in lines 24–5?
   c) Explain whether you think these unusual combinations are effective.
7 Do you think the last three lines constitute a vivid ending to the poem? What is your reaction to the image that the poet uses?
8 Write a short paragraph explaining whether or not this poem appeals to you. Refer closely to lines and phrases that illustrate the points you want to make.

27 On a Friend's Escape from Drowning off the Norfolk Coast

Came up that cold sea at Cromer like a running grave
    Beside him as he struck
Wildly towards the shore, but the blackcapped wave
    Crossed him and swung him back,
5 And he saw his son digging in the castled dirt that could save.
    Then the farewell rock
Rose a last time to his eyes. As he cried out
    A pawing gag of the sea
Smothered his cry and he sank in his own shout
10   Like a dying airman. Then she
Deep near her son asleep on the hourglass sand
    Was wakened by whom
Save the Fate who knew that this was the wrong time:
    And opened her eyes

15 On the death of her son's begetter. Up she flies
     Into the hydra-headed
   Grave as he closes his life upon her who for
     Life has so richly bedded him.
   But she drove through his drowning like Orpheus and tore
20   Back by the hair
   Her escaping bridegroom. And on the sand their son
     Stood laughing where
   He was almost an orphan. Then the three lay down
     On that cold sand,
25 Each holding the other by a living hand.

1 Outline in your own words the situation described in the first four lines.

2 Explain the reference to 'the blackcapped wave' (line 3).

3 What is meant by 'the castled dirt' (line 5)?

4 a) Explain the point of the metaphor used in line 8.
b) How is it carried on in line 9?

5 What is the significance of the expression 'the hourglass sand' (line 11)?

6 What explanation is given of the fact that the wife woke at the precise moment her husband was drowning?

7 In Greek mythology Orpheus went down to the Underworld to rescue his wife, Eurydice. In what way is the situation here similar and in what way is it different?

8 Do you think the boy fully understands the position in lines 21–23? Give your reasons.

9 In your opinion, which is the most significant word in the last line? Why is this?

10 Explain what effect the poet might be trying to achieve by his use of alternate long and short lines.

28 a   The Soldier

If I should die, think only this of me
    That there's some corner of a foreign field
That is for ever England. There shall be
    In that rich earth a richer dust concealed;
5 A dust that England bore, shaped, made aware,
    Gave, once, her flowers to love, her ways to roam,
A body of England's, breathing English air,
    Washed by the rivers, blest by suns of home.
And think, this heart, all evil shed away,
10   A pulse in the eternal mind, no less
Gives somewhere back the thoughts by England given;
    Her sights and sounds; dreams, happy as her day;
And laughter, learnt of friends; and gentleness,
    In hearts at peace, under an English heaven.

1 In what circumstances was this poem written, do you think?
2 Which words run like a refrain through the poem? What effect
   does this repetition have?
3 a) What is the 'richer dust' referred to in line 4?
   b) Why should it be thought of as being richer?
4 a) What symbol is used to represent the finer part of the poet's
      being?
   b) Which word carries on the same idea and how is it particularly
      appropriate?

28 b   Why Patriots Are a Bit Nuts in the Head

Patriots are a bit nuts in the head
because they wear
red, white and blue-
tinted spectacles
5 (red for blood
white for glory

and blue ...
for a boy)
and are in effervescent danger
10   of losing their lives
lives are good for you
when you are alive
you can eat and drink a lot
and go out with girls
15   (sometimes if you are lucky
      you can even go to bed with them)
but you can't do this
if you have your belly shot away
and your seeds
20   spread over some corner of a foreign field
to facilitate
in later years
the growing of oats by some peasant yobbo

when you are posthumous it is cold and dark
25 and that is why patriots are a bit nuts in the head

5 Express in more formal language what the poet means by line 1.
6 What is the usual significance of 'red, white and blue' (line 3)?
7 Of which well-known phrase is 'red, white and blue-tinted spectacles' an echo?
8 Why do you think line 11 is printed in italics?
9 What does 'posthumous' mean (line 24)? Why do you think this word was used rather than a simpler one?
10 Concentrating on subject-matter, form and language, explain in detail what these two poems have in common and in what ways they differ.
11 a) What are the two attitudes to dying for one's country presented in 'The Soldier' and 'Why Patriots Are a Bit Nuts in the Head'?
    b) Which of the two points of view do you think is expressed more effectively?
    c) With which viewpoint do you have more sympathy? Give your reasons.

29 High Wood

Ladies and gentlemen, this is High Wood,
Called by the French, Bois de Fourneaux,
The famous spot which in Nineteen-Sixteen,
July, August and September was the scene
5 Of long and bitterly contested strife,
By reason of its High commanding site.
Observe the effect of shell-fire in the trees
Standing and fallen; here is wire; this trench
For months inhabited, twelve times changed hands;
10 (They soon fall in), used later as a grave.
It has been said on good authority
That in the fighting for this patch of wood
Were killed somewhere above eight thousand men,
Of whom the greater part were buried here,
15 This mound on which you stand being . . .
                                Madame, please,
You are requested kindly not to touch
Or take away the Company's property
As souvenirs; you'll find we have on sale
20 A large variety, all guaranteed.
As I was saying, all is as it was,
This is an unknown British officer,
The tunic having lately rotted off.
Please follow me – this way . . .
25   the *path*, sir, *please*,
The ground which was secured at great expense
The Company keeps absolutely untouched,
And in that dug-out (genuine) we provide
Refreshments at a reasonable rate.
30 You are requested not to leave about
Paper, or ginger-beer bottles, or orange-peel,
There are waste-paper baskets at the gate.

1 What is the imaginary narrator of this poem doing?
2 Why was the site described strategically important?
3 What, can we infer, was the narrator about to say in line 15?

4 Why did he break off what he was saying?
5 What causes the second interruption in line 24?
6 Explain in full what you have learned about the Company mentioned in lines 18 and 27.
7 Quote one detail from the poem which seems to you to create a particularly powerful effect and then explain the reason for its impact.
8 Reading between the lines, as we say, what do you believe would be the poet's own attitude to the activities of the fictitious Company described here? What leads you to your conclusion?
9 a) What, in your opinion, prompted the poet to write 'High Wood'?

b) In what ways has his poem confirmed or contradicted your own impressions of the Great War of 1914–18?

30 Bread and a Pension

It was not our duty to question but to guard,
maintaining order; see that none escaped
who may be required for questioning by the State.
The price was bread and a pension and not a hard
life on the whole. Some even scraped
enough on the side to build up a fairish estate

for the day of retirement. I never could
understand the complaints of the restless ones
who found the hours long, time dragging;
it always does. The old hands knew how good
the guardroom fire could be, the guns
gleaming against the wall and the nagging

wind like a wife – outside. There were cards
for such occasions and good companions
who truly were more than home since they shared
one's working life without difference or hard words,
aimed at much the same thing, and shared opinions
on news they read. If they cared

much it was for the quiet life. You cannot hold
that against them, since it's roundly human
and any decent man would want it the same.
For these were decent: did as they were told,
fed prisoners, buried the dead, and, on occasion,
loaded the deathcart with those who were sent to the flames.

1 To judge from the first few lines of this poem, who is the narrator
and what does his job appear to be?
2 a) What is his attitude to his job?
  b) How did his attitude differ from that of some of his
     colleagues?
3 a) Which of the details mentioned in the second stanza seems to
     you to be the most significant for a full understanding of the
     poem?
  b) What is the reason for this?
4 Explain in your own words what the narrator liked about his
working conditions.
5 What can you infer from the poem about the narrator's home
life?
6 a) What is the implication in the last line?
  b) Why does the poet leave this detail to the end, do you think?
  c) Explain whether it modifies your impression of the narrator.
7 a) Summarize the argument put forward by the narrator of this
     poem.
  b) Show the relevance of the title to his argument.
  c) Explain, with reasons, whether or not you find his case
     convincing.
8 Write a short paragraph on the use of rhyme in the poem. (Does
it have any pattern? What effect does it have? Is its use
appropriate to the subject?)

31   Five Ways to Kill a Man

There are many cumbersome ways to kill a man.
You can make him carry a plank of wood
to the top of a hill and nail him to it. To do this
properly you require a crowd of people
5 wearing sandals, a cock that crows, a cloak
to dissect, a sponge, some vinegar and one
man to hammer the nails home.

Or you can take a length of steel,
shaped and chased in a traditional way,
10 and attempt to pierce the metal cage he wears.
But for this you need white horses,
English trees, men with bows and arrows,
at least two flags, a prince, and a
castle to hold your banquet in.

15 Dispensing with nobility, you may, if the wind
allows, blow gas at him. But then you need
a mile of mud sliced through with ditches,
not to mention black boots, bomb craters,
more mud, a plague of rats, a dozen songs
20 and some round hats made of steel.

In an age of aeroplanes, you may fly
miles above your victim and dispose of him by
pressing one small switch. All you then
require is an ocean to separate you, two
25 systems of government, a nation's scientists,
several factories, a psychopath and
land that no-one needs for several years.

These are, as I began, cumbersome ways
to kill a man. Simpler, direct, and much more neat
30 is to see that he is living somewhere in the middle
of the twentieth century, and leave him there.

1 a) What is the poet referring to in lines 2–3?
   b) Explain the significance of each of the further details given in
   lines 4—7.
2 Write a short paragraph explaining all the allusions in the second
   stanza.
3 a) What is the poet describing in the third stanza?
   b) Explain the references to i) 'a mile of mud'; ii) 'a dozen songs';
   iii) 'some round hats made of steel'.
4 a) In what way does the fourth method of killing a man differ
   from the three previously mentioned?
   b) What is meant by
       'land that no-one needs for several years' (line 27)?
5 a) Say in your own words what implication is made in the last
   section.
   b) Why do you think the poet has made this section shorter than
   the others?
6 Write a paragraph commenting on the mood and tone of this
   poem.
7 Give your reaction to the style in which this poem is written. In
   particular, comment on the use made of accumulated details and
   alllusions.

Useful Critical Terms

alliteration: the repetition of consonants in words and phrases to give particular emphasis, e.g. 'the cool colonnade', 'the perishing pleasures of man' ('The Poplar Field', p. 14).

allusion: a reference to a person, character or event often by way of a parallel, e.g. the mention of Orpheus in 'On a Friend's Escape from Drowning' (p. 42) is a classical allusion, i.e. a reference to an event in Greek mythology.

assonance: the repetition of vowel sounds to gain special effects, e.g. 'clowning and clouting', 'shouting and pouting' ('Jigsaw II', p. 28).

compare: show the similarities – usually in a comparison of two poems.

compound words: double-barrelled words made by combining two existing words. They are sometimes used to pile up effects in descriptive poems, e.g. 'wind-wandering, weed-winding bank' ('Binsey Poplars', p. 15).

consonants: all the letters of the alphabet except the five vowels.

context: the place or circumstances in which a particular word or phrase is used. When the meaning of a word has to be explained, it is always within its context, i.e., as used in this instance.

contrast: show the differences; often linked with *compare*.

diction: the poet's language, the words that he chooses. It may be simple, modern, old-fashioned, etc.

figures of speech: devices employed by writers to make their work more vivid and found particularly in poetry. The most frequently used are *similes, metaphors, alliteration* and *onomatopoeia*.

form: the shape or pattern in which a poet presents his material. Some poems are continuous, written in one piece; others are divided into regular stanzas; others seem to follow no set pattern and are written in what is called free verse.

free verse: poetry which seems to have no pattern and does not conform to set stanzas or rhyme schemes. It is popular with contemporary poets and is typical of the modern movement in all the arts away from conventions and restrictions. An ex-ample in this collection is 'Why Patriots Are a Bit Nuts in the Head' (p. 43).

images: sense-impressions which poets use to set their readers' or listeners' imaginations working. Images contribute to the richness of poetry because they not only create pictures in the mind's eye but can also appeal to the other senses, e.g., 'the corner where it was always dusk/And equatorial, aromatic with coffee beans' – smell ('Jones the Grocer', p. 10); 'Our slamming voices must seem crude' – sound ('Hedgehog', p. 22); 'his hands cold with death' – touch ('Life-Saver', p. 40).

infer: deduce, work out. Poets often work indirectly, by hints and suggestions rather than by making direct statements. We have to read between the lines, as it were, make our own *inferences* and draw our own conclusions.

literal: applied to words used in their everyday, primary sense. The opposite of metaphorical or figurative.

metaphors: used frequently by poets, they make us think of familiar objects in a new way. They suggest similarities by describing one thing in terms usually associated with another and not literally true, e.g. a thrush is said to have 'black *pebble-eyes*' ('The Thrush's Nest', p. 16); and the dammed-up waters of the Nile are called 'a bank of the country's blood' ('Egypt', p. 29). Some metaphors can be sustained over several lines, e.g. in 'The Mirror' (p. 39) the mirror is thought of in the second stanza as a lake and this idea is developed over nine lines.

metre: see also rhythm. When the weak and strong stresses in a line of poetry conform to a regular pattern or beat, we have a definite metre. Several basic patterns are used in English verse, but their study is too technical for this book.

mood: the overall feeling generated by a poem. It may be happy, sad, optimistic, disillusioned, etc.

narrator: the person who is imagined as 'speaking' the poem. We cannot always assume that it is the poet himself who is presenting his own point of view, and the term *narrator* is a convenient one, even if very often the poem does not tell a story.

onomatopoeia: a foreign-looking word (it comes from Greek) and hard to spell. It means the use of words whose sound echoes the sense they are conveying, e.g.

'A rifle's ringing crack

Split their Arcadia wide open' ('The Sabbath', p. 24).
The short, sharp words 'crack' and 'split' and the alliterative r's effectively echo a sudden rifle shot.

personification: the term used when something which is not human is thought of in human terms, e.g. in the poem 'I am Jamaica' (p. 26) the country is given the identity of a mother and in 'Life-Saver' (p. 40) there is a reference to 'thin brother Death'.

prose: ordinary writing as used in letters, newspapers and books. It rarely has the concentrated power and rhythm of poetry.

refrain: a line or lines repeated, possibly with slight variations, several times in the course of a poem; less obvious, perhaps, than a chorus in a song. The nearest approaches to refrains in this book can be found in 'Jigsaw II' (p. 28) and 'The Lament of the Banana Man' (p. 24).

rhyme: the repetition of sounds, usually at the end of lines. Remember that it is the *sound* which determines whether words rhyme and not the spelling. When there is a definite pattern it is called a rhyme-scheme. Rhyme is not essential to poetry and much modern verse dispenses with it altogether.

rhythm: all spoken language has rhythm; in poetry rhythmic patterns are more pronounced, making a vital contribution to the total effect of the poem. The rhythm of a poem is carried along by the pattern of stresses in the lines. It is a complex thing, dependent upon such factors as the length of line and the stresses within individual words. It is roughly equivalent to the 'beat' in music, but often, especially in modern poems, its influence is very subtle and hard to isolate. For a poem with obvious, traditional, measured rhythm see 'The Poplar Field' (p. 14) and for a typical modern approach see 'Early Morning Feed' (p. 6).

senses: the five senses of sight, hearing, smell, taste and touch. All poetry needs an imaginative response and much of the impact of descriptive poetry in particular is made through the senses.

similes: direct comparisons between two things which are alike in one particular way. By using similes, poets add an extra dimension to their writing, especially if the nature of the comparison is unexpected, e.g.

'The snail moves
Like a hovercraft
Held up by a rubber
Cushion of itself.'

          'Hedgehog' (p. 21).

We would not normally associate snails with hovercraft – they are different in so many ways – but they do have in common their 'rubber skirt'. Similes, incidentally, are easier to spot than metaphors because the two sides of the comparison are always linked by the word *like* (see above) or *as*, e.g.

'His hands white and soft as the lard he stacked
In small meticulous rows' ('Jones the Grocer', p. 10).

stanzas: the sections into which some poems are divided, popularly known as verses. Stanzas have set numbers of lines ranging usually from two to nine.

symbols: objects which, as well as being significant in their own right, are chosen to stand for, or represent, ideas or abstractions on a higher level, e.g. in 'Child of our Time' (p. 3) 'the wounded moon' and 'the travelling star' symbolize the advance of science into space.

theme: the central idea of a poem, the 'message' the poet may be trying to put across. Some poems have more obvious themes than others which concentrate on building up impressions; e.g. 'The Sabbath' (p. 23) has a more distinct theme than '4C Boy' (p. 8).

tone: another word for *mood*, already defined.

vowels: *a, e, i, o* and *u* – the five letters that are not consonants.

Poems and Poets